Small Things with Great Love

with

Great Love

A 9-Day Novena
to Mother Teresa,
Saint of the Gutters

DONNA-MARIE COOPER O'BOYLE

PARACLETE PRESS
BREWSTER, MASSACHUSETTS

2019 First printing

*Small Things with Great Love: A 9-Day Novena to
Mother Teresa, Saint of the Gutters*

Copyright © 2019 by Donna-Marie Cooper O'Boyle

ISBN 978-1-64060-113-0

Scripture quotations are from New Revised Standard Version Bible:
Catholic Edition, copyright © 1989, 1993 National Council of the
Churches of Christ in the United States of America. Used by permission.
All rights reserved.

The Paraclete Press name and logo (dove on cross) are trademarks of
Paraclete Press, Inc.

Library of Congress Cataloging-in-Publication
Names: O'Boyle, Donna-Marie Cooper, author.
Title: Small things with great love : a 9-day novena to Mother Teresa, Saint
    of the Gutters / Donna-Marie Cooper O'Boyle.
Description: Brewster, Massachusetts : Paraclete Press, [2019] | Series:
    9 days of prayer to change your life | Includes bibliographical references.
Identifiers: LCCN 2018031180 | ISBN 9781640601130 (trade paper)
Subjects: LCSH: Teresa, Mother, Saint, 1910-1997—Prayers and
    devotions. | Jesus Christ--Devotional literature. | Novenas. | Teresa,
    Mother, Saint,   1910-1997—Quotations.
Classification: LCC BX2167.T38 O26 2019 | DDC 271/.97—dc23LC
record available at https://lccn.loc.gov/2018031180

10 9 8 7 6 5 4 3 2 1

Published by Paraclete Press
Brewster, Massachusetts
www.paracletepress.com

Printed in the United States of America

contents

preface

Catholics have been praying novenas through-out the ages. Specifically, a novena is a special prayer or spiritual exercise to inspire faith. Novena in Latin means "nine." Usually, a novena consists of a prayer that is prayed for nine days for specific intentions, sometimes invoking the intercession of a particular saint. Mother Teresa often prayed what she called an "express novena" of nine Memorares ("Remember, O most gracious Virgin Mary. . .") in a row for an urgent need.

Why nine days? The significance of the number nine has been woven throughout history. For instance, in medieval times, a sum of nine Masses was the usual protocol after a death for the repose of the soul. The number nine also comes into play for popes, since it is commonplace to observe nine days of mourning after a pope's death.

In addition, consider what happened when Jesus walked the earth. At the Ascension, Jesus entrusted his apostles with the Great Commission, telling them to return to Jerusalem and wait for the coming of the Holy Spirit. We read about praying for nine days in the Acts of the Apostles. "After that they returned to Jerusalem from the mount called Olivet near Jerusalem—a mere Sabbath's journey away. Together they devoted themselves to constant prayer" (Acts 1:12, 14). Exactly nine days later, the Holy Spirit descended upon the apostles and Mary at Pentecost. The apostles' nine-day period of active prayer is at the heart of a novena.

It is essential to keep in mind that when praying a novena, we should be sincere and devout, remembering God, who in his goodness answers all our prayers according to his holy will. Therefore, a novena is not some kind of magical formula or a superstitious practice, in which by saying a prayer for nine days, we will receive our wish. No, not at all. A novena is a beautiful tradition of prayer in the Catholic Church that is meant to inspire our faith.

In *Small Things with Great Love: A 9-Day Novena to Mother Teresa, Saint of the Gutters* we invoke the intercession of Saint Mother Teresa of Calcutta for our urgent, as well as our lesser needs—big and small. She will help!

one

One at a Time

> " The biggest disease today is not leprosy
> or tuberculosis, but rather the feeling
> of being unwanted, uncared for and
> deserted by everybody."
> —Mother Teresa

There's no doubt about it. We simply cannot lasso time and force it to stand still. It's impossible. We live in a fast-paced world that seems to move faster by the day. Our modern technology accelerates at such a clip that computers, mobile phones, and other devices become obsolete or antiquated every time we turn around. Unless we are hermits living in a cave somewhere, our lives are an inevitable whirlwind of activity. (I know monks and nuns who even struggle with this.) We rush from one activity to the next—without too much thought about what we might have missed had we paused to take in the moment instead of rushing to the next experience. Could we be missing an important encounter? Could we have lost the opportunity to help someone in a transforming way?

Time is a precious commodity. It's something we need to exist, something we hate to part with, yet something we intensely waste. Truth be told, Mother Teresa couldn't lasso time either. However, time surely seemed to stand still when that saint of the gutters gazed into your eyes. I was a very fortunate recipient of those beautiful gazes on many occasions.

Mother Teresa paused to take care of every single need that unfolded before her—whether it was the beggar at her door, picking maggots off the person she found struggling in the gutter, feeding and rocking the tiny baby she found discarded in a dust bin, or negotiating a ceasefire between political enemies. She even paused from her busy schedule in caring for the poor to talk with me, a suburban housewife. Furthermore, she stayed in touch with me over the next ten years in visits, letters, and even a phone call between the States and Calcutta. Mother Teresa took the time—she cared—she loved with Christ's love. She was committed to caring for each need—one at a time. Every single person was important to her. Each was "Jesus in the distressing disguise of the poorest of the poor," those to whom Jesus referred as the "least." Jesus said, "Whatever you do to the least of my brothers, you do to me." We might ask ourselves, "What are we doing or not doing to Jesus?" We will be answering these questions on our Judgment Day.

One Person at a Time

Each person and each experience is important. Mother Teresa didn't jump up on the nearest table or climb to the rooftop to shout out the Gospels to masses of people. Most of her evangelization was accomplished one-on-one—with each person she encountered. She saw Jesus in everyone and treated each person with love. She strove with all her heart to follow God's will. She trusted that God would reveal it to her. She walked forward in faith even when it was extremely difficult, when she could no longer hear God's call to her heart or feel his consolations after she crossed over the threshold to the slums of Calcutta when she experienced a severe dark night in the spiritual life. Mother Teresa continued to smile and kept on taking care of those whom God placed in her life. She was absolutely sure that she needed to satiate Jesus's thirst for souls by caring for the poor and the "least." She prayed much and asked God to let her light shine through the darkness to lead others to heaven.

In 1982, in the middle of the war in Lebanon, one hundred disabled and ill children were left without care, abandoned in an orphanage in Beirut due to their shelter having been bombed. Mother Teresa wanted to rescue them. In an attempt to make her aware of the dangers, officials asked her if she could hear the bombs.

They said it was too risky—a priest had been killed by bombs just two weeks prior. Mother Teresa assured them that she wasn't worried—that there would be a ceasefire the following day in which they could rescue the children. With whom did she negotiate a ceasefire? They wanted to know. The Mother of God! Mother Teresa had asked for it in prayer and was certain the Blessed Mother would deliver it to them on the eve of her feast day (the Assumption). Officials explained that it was absolutely impossible to safely make the short journey to reach those children. The determined little nun answered, "All for Jesus. You see, I've always seen things in this light. A long time ago, when I picked up the first person [from a street in Calcutta], if I had not done it that first time, I would not have picked up 42,000 after that. One at a time. . . ." The officials then agreed to help her with the rescue if the fighting stopped as she predicted. An unreal silence enveloped the city the following day. The fighting stopped completely. Officials were amazed. Mother Teresa rescued all the hungry children and brought them to a Christian suburb of Beirut.

Mother Teresa was very small in stature, even frail in some respects, and she was a woman—the supposed "weaker sex." However, this petite woman's "yes" to God truly changed the world forever! She opened the world's eyes to our duty to feed the hungry and clothe the naked, and she told us that a far worse hunger exists in the Western world. People there are starving for love and kindness. Mother Teresa said, "The biggest disease today is not leprosy or tuberculosis, but rather the feeling of being unwanted, uncared for and deserted by everybody." This one woman's "yes" shows us that our own "yes" can be just as important. With God's grace, each person's "yes" to God will work miracles!

Our Lord calls us all not merely to get to heaven by the skin of our teeth one day, but to bring countless souls with us by our lives of love. God calls us to evangelize in a variety of ways throughout our days in all our states of life. We do this one by one— ministering to each need as it unfolds before us.

Don't Miss the Opportunity

I would guess that many of us continually miss out on clear opportunities to carry out works of mercy, fixated as we are on rushing to the next activity and wasting time on senseless activities. We all do this. We waste time by staying on the Internet too long, watching too much television, and otherwise entertaining ourselves. We should ponder this. We need to get our priorities straight, as well as slow down and love one another.

I am reminded of something my sister Barbara said as she lay in her bed dying of cancer. Her eyelids were often heavy and falling. She was so tired from the side effects of strong medicines, her body fighting hard to stay alive. She struggled to keep her eyes open. "I don't want to miss anything," she told me. She died just a few days later. Let us be attentive, use our time wisely, and prayerfully care for the needs in our midst.

reflect

Take time to ponder your life. Are you in too much of a hurry? Can you take concrete steps to slow down and live within the present moments of your life so as to be more attentive to needs around you? Perhaps you can put this on your "to-do" list and then make it happen. At least three times a day, pause and immerse yourself right into your present moment. Bless yourself with the powerful Sign of the Cross. Offer God a simple heartfelt prayer: *Jesus, help me to live in this moment. Jesus, I trust in you!* Try not to worry about yesterday or tomorrow. Live right now. What could God be asking you in this moment? After a while, you will be more able to consciously stop and pray, and to become aware of the moment. Ask Mother Teresa to help you to be more aware of needs in those present moments, as well as to listen to God's whispers to your soul. Now pray the novena prayer.

Novena
prayer

St. Teresa of Calcutta, please hear my prayer. You are a faithful and devoted servant of our Lord and of his poor—those you called "The poorest of the poor," those in the greatest need, and those for whom our Lord instructs us to serve, saying, "Whatever you do to the least of my brothers you do to me." Through your life of holy service, you demonstrated the joy of loving and taught us the greatness and dignity of every human being, from conception to natural death. Your continual walk in faith to serve those in need even as you were stricken with hardship and darkness floods my soul with great hope. Please, dear Saint of the Gutters, help me in my present need by presenting my prayer petition before the throne of God.

[Here, mention your request.]

Please also intercede for me so that I may have the strength and courage to give my own personal "yes" each day and that I will come closer to our divine Lord Jesus Christ, ultimately joining you one day in praising him forever in heaven.

Amen.

two

Small Things with Great Love

> " Do ordinary things with extraordinary love."
> —Mother Teresa

Mother Teresa had a great love for the other most popular saint of the twentieth century, St. Therese of Lisieux, the saint of the "Little Way," affectionately called the "Little Flower." She modeled herself after her, often preaching about the "little way" of doing things. Mother Teresa was famous for saying, "Do ordinary things with extraordinary love." She meant we should put our hearts wholeheartedly into all that we do. When love is involved, *little* things might not be so little after all. Something quite ordinary can become miraculous when carried out with extraordinary love. This doesn't mean that the "great love" we put into the "small thing" we are doing is going to *feel* extraordinary, or "warm and fuzzy," or that it will even seem significant. Many times, it will seem quite mundane and unimportant. Yet, within those ordinary things, an awful lot can happen. Believe it or not, we can even put "great love" into cleaning a toilet! Truly. Allow me to explain.

One time when Mother Teresa was visiting one of the Missionaries of Charity convents, she came out of the bathroom with a big smile on her face. A sister there inquired about her expression of happiness. Mother Teresa remarked that some sister there obviously really loved our Lord! Why? She said the bathroom was sparkling clean!

Mother Teresa taught her sisters well. She encouraged them to do everything for Jesus, and of course to do small things with great love. Cleaning a toilet is not typically viewed as something to be proud about. You don't need college degrees to accomplish it. But, you do need a loving heart if you want to please Jesus.

Though a nun, Mother Teresa was no stranger to modern-day problems, as well as the horrid conditions in the slums of Calcutta where she ministered so often to the "poorest of the poor." She said, "The greatest evil is the lack of love and charity, the terrible indifference toward one's neighbor who lives at the roadside, assaulted by exploitation, corruption, poverty and disease." This hero of the poor was often drawing attention to the needs of the disadvantaged in the Western world. She encouraged people to reach out beyond their comfort zones to bring Christ's love to those starving for love. Amazingly, our little acts of love can be transforming in their lives and in ours, too.

A small thing done with great love can be a warm smile for someone who might feel troubled or unloved. God works miracles through our humble efforts.

Simple Smiles

Once, after speaking at a conference, I had to walk to the back of the room to do a book signing. As I made my way there, I happened to smile at a man standing alone on the side of the room. He later wrote to me to say that my smile had totally transformed his heart. I never could have imagined that would be the case. We might never know the transforming power and beauty in our warm reaching out to others.

Mother Teresa encouraged people to smile. She said it was a way to peace. She also said we should smile at those to whom we might not be particularly fond. "Peace begins with a smile," she said. "Smile five times a day at someone you don't really want to smile at; do it for peace." St. Therese said something similar: "Without love, deeds, even the most brilliant, count as nothing." We know from the biography of the saint of the "Little Way" that she used to smile often at a cranky old nun in her convent. St. Therese's warm, loving smiles eventually won over the nun's heart.

I received an unexpected email one day from someone I hadn't heard from in about forty years. Turns out she had seen my posts on social media and decided to email an article on prayer she thought I'd like. I suddenly realized who the woman was (since her last name is different now that she is married). I was more than a bit stunned when it registered in my brain. She was one of a group of young teen girls who had ganged up on me in junior high school with an abusive note that upset me very much. I read her email further and was absolutely amazed at her words. She told me my smiles to her in the school hallways were a saving grace, back then, counteracting the piercing bad comments and bullying she received from those who thought her "stuck up" or arrogant. In fact, she was just desperately shy. This woman's unexpected words impacted my heart, knowing all these years later that God had used me to comfort her.

Pressing on with Great Love

Mother Teresa told the story of how her heart was deeply impacted by a simple generous act from a poor man who knocked on her door one evening. She had just been awarded the Nobel Peace Prize, and the man wanted to give her something. He opened his hand to reveal a minuscule amount of money. Mother Teresa was torn because she knew he needed the money to live, but she also knew that he was trying to make a sacrifice and do a small thing with great love. Mother Teresa decided to accept his meager gift and an immediate, joyful radiance spread over the man's face. To Mother Teresa, the man's tiny contribution became like tens of thousands of dollars—because it was given with great love and sacrifice.

It might not be easy for us to do ordinary things with extraordinary love. Most days we are in a rush and want to hurry to check off our "to-do" lists. We don't put in the extra effort. We might also think that those ordinary things are, well, just *ordinary*. Yet, many graces abound in the mystery of the ordinary when our hearts open and we give with great love.

reflect

Take time to ponder your life. Can you put greater effort into your actions? Even cleaning a toilet, for instance?

Through the enormity of her work, Mother Teresa remained "small." Her great humility and smallness were the secrets of her great sanctity. The Saint of the Gutters tells us that Jesus is pleased with the love we put into our actions and in serving others. She said, "Let us keep very small and follow the Little Flower's way of trust, love, and joy, and we will fulfill Mother's promise to give Saints to Mother Church." Ask Mother Teresa to show you how to transform seemingly insignificant things into something very meaningful and loving. Now, pray the novena prayer.

Novena
prayer

St. Teresa of Calcutta, please hear my prayer. You are a faithful and devoted servant of our Lord and of his poor—those you called "The poorest of the poor," those in the greatest need, and those for whom our Lord instructs us to serve, saying, "Whatever you do to the least of my brothers you do to me." Through your life of holy service, you demonstrated the joy of loving and taught us the greatness and dignity of every human being, from conception to natural death. Your continual walk in faith to serve those in need even as you were stricken with hardship and darkness floods my soul with great hope. Please, dear Saint of the Gutters, help me in my present need by presenting my prayer petition before the throne of God.

[Here, mention your request.]

Please also intercede for me so that I may have the strength and courage to give my own personal "yes" each day and that I will come closer to our divine Lord Jesus Christ, ultimately joining you one day in praising him forever in heaven.

Amen.

three

The Thirst of Jesus

" I thirst."
—Jesus, when hanging from the Cross

Remarkably, Jesus thirsts for our love! The thirst of Jesus is a powerful thing.

How does the thirst of Jesus relate to Mother Teresa? Let's go back again to the time when Jesus walked the earth. In the Gospel of John, we become aware that the mystery of prayer is revealed by the well where one goes to seek water. We learn the story of the Samaritan woman unexpectedly meeting the Lord Jesus at Jacob's well in an ordinary, yet extraordinary encounter. The woman wanted to collect water for her family, and Jesus was there at the well to offer his living water to her—*specifically*. There, beside the well, a fascinating and revealing conversation between a Samaritan woman and Our Lord Jesus Christ was launched.

Incidentally, chatting by the well at that time was no doubt a highlight of a woman's day. But, this Samaritan woman, who was most likely ostracized and labeled as immoral by the other women because she was openly living with a man, the sixth in a series of men, so we are told, came along to the well at high noon, the hottest part of the day. We venture to guess this was to avoid others. But, we shall see that Jesus knew when he would find her there. First, of course, we recognize that Jesus asked the woman for a drink. He was speaking to a woman out in public, something totally unheard of at that time. Second, we see that the woman was a Samaritan, and Samaritans were despised by the Jews. Yet Jesus persisted with his loving confrontation, asking the woman about her husband. The woman hemmed and hawed and sidestepped the issue to disguise her sinful life. She focused on the law—"You are a Jew, and I am a Samaritan. . . ." However, Jesus focused on grace and love. In a matter of time, though, by God's grace, she recognized with whom she was speaking and suddenly began to understand the deep love of her Savior and his insatiable thirst for mankind. The Samaritan woman's heart was immediately transformed, and she became a missionary, leaving her bucket behind, and running back to her village to bring to her people the incredible holy message of our Lord's love and of his living water. She absolutely needed to share what she had received!

St. Augustine described this remarkable and historic meeting between the Samaritan woman and Jesus, telling us that Jesus comes to meet every human being and finds us as we are drawing our water.

Interpreting this scenario as one that touches us all, not just the Samaritan woman, St. Augustine explains that Jesus is the first to seek us. Jesus's request for a drink expresses his thirst for our love. He loves each one of us, including the sinner!

Augustine tells us that the desire that Jesus has for our love "arises from the depths of God's desire for us." We can read about this in the *Catechism of the Catholic Church*. Augustine explained that even though we do not realize it, "Prayer is the encounter of God's thirst with ours. God thirsts that we may thirst for Him" (CCC, 2560). This profound insight gives us a new way to view prayer: amazingly, God thirsts for us and wants us to thirst for him! He seeks us out and calls us to a special union with himself.

Later, Jesus profoundly thirsted from the Cross. Our Lord uttered those two powerful words, "I thirst," as he hung on the Cross, dying for our salvation. His thirst was not for water but rather for our love. Pope Francis spoke about this thirst of our Savior. He said, "Gathered before Jesus crucified, we hear His words ring out also for us: 'I thirst" (Jn 19:28). Thirst, more than hunger, is the greatest need of humanity and also its greatest suffering. Let us contemplate then the mystery of Almighty God, who in his mercy became poor among men. What does the Lord thirst for?" The pontiff asked. "Certainly for water, that element essential for life. But above all for love, that element no less essential for living. He thirsts to give us the living waters of His love, but also to receive our love."

Mother Teresa and the Thirst of Jesus

Mother Teresa often spoke about how Jesus thirsts for our love. The humble saint of the gutters experienced Jesus's thirst in a mystical way. She heard Jesus calling her to give her life in service of the poor and the rejected, those she called "the poorest of the poor." In doing so, she would satiate Jesus's thirst. Mother Teresa lived her life striving to satiate his thirst by taking care of the "least" all over this planet. I was often blessed to see this remarkable holy woman in action. I have also observed such a deep reverence and understanding of our Savior's thirst in all the Missionaries of Charity sisters that I have met. Mother Teresa insisted that the aim of the Missionaries of Charity was "to satiate the thirst of Jesus."

Mother Teresa reflected on those two powerful words in a letter to her sisters. "At this most difficult time He proclaimed, 'I thirst.' And people thought He was thirsty in an ordinary way and they gave Him vinegar straight away; but it was not for that thirst; it was for our love, our affection, that intimate attachment to Him, and that sharing of His passion. He used, 'I thirst,' instead of 'Give Me your love'. . . 'I thirst.' Let us hear Him saying it to me and saying it to you."

On another occasion, when Mother Teresa was invited to give an address at the National Prayer Breakfast in 1994, she brought up the subject of the thirst of Jesus. "When He was dying on the Cross, Jesus said, 'I thirst.' Jesus is thirsting for our love, and this is the thirst of everyone, poor and rich alike." She continued, "We all thirst for the love of others, that they go out of their way to avoid harming us and to do good to us. This is the meaning of true love, to give until it hurts."

The words "I Thirst" mark every Missionaries of Charity chapel throughout the world. I was blessed to be inside many of them. Those words are painted on the wall beside the tabernacle, near the altar, because Mother Teresa wanted to remind all who enter the chapel of Jesus's thirst for our love and that we need to thirst for his love too. Incredible! Jesus thirsts for our love. Take time to ponder that.

reflect

Toward the end of her life, Mother Teresa wrote a letter to her sisters. She wrote, "Why does Jesus say 'I Thirst'? What does it mean? . . . If you remember anything from Mother's letter, remember this — 'I Thirst' is something much deeper than just Jesus saying 'I love you.' Until you know deep inside that Jesus thirsts for you — you can't begin to know who He wants to be for you. Or who He wants you to be for Him." Mother Teresa wanted her sisters to deeply ponder the great mystery of Jesus profoundly thirsting for them. She mentioned herself in the third person as she often did in her expressive letters and teachings to her spiritual daughters. Ponder Mother's words and pray the novena prayer.

Novena
prayer

St. Teresa of Calcutta, please hear my prayer. You are a faithful and devoted servant of our Lord and of his poor—those you called "The poorest of the poor," those in the greatest need, and those for whom our Lord instructs us to serve, saying, "Whatever you do to the least of my brothers you do to me." Through your life of holy service, you demonstrated the joy of loving and taught us the greatness and dignity of every human being, from conception to natural death. Your continual walk in faith to serve those in need even as you were stricken with hardship and darkness floods my soul with great hope. Please, dear Saint of the Gutters, help me in my present need by presenting my prayer petition before the throne of God.

[Here, mention your request.]

Please also intercede for me so that I may have the strength and courage to give my own personal "yes" each day and that I will come closer to our divine Lord Jesus Christ, ultimately joining you one day in praising him forever in heaven.

Amen.

four

"You did it to Me"

" Just as you did it to one of the least of these
who are members of the family,
you did it to me."
—Jesus, in Matthew 25:40

Mother Teresa was a pious nun, very close to our Lord, but she was also a woman on the go. She proclaimed, "Love is not words. It is action. Our vocation is to love." This little nun got things done! Certainly, moss did not grow under her feet. This seemingly tireless woman, who was approaching old age, was out of bed before the other sisters who rose at 4:40 a.m. to wash, dress, and meet in the chapel by 5:00 a.m. for prayers before 6:00 a.m. Mass. The daily schedule consisted of prayer and work, simple meals, and a half hour of recreation each evening.

Mother Teresa, who was so in love with Jesus, was passionate about following him and loving him, emulating the great saints who had come before. She wanted to say "yes" to whatever God expected of her. She explained that she "wanted to give God something very beautiful" and "without reserve." As a Sister of Loretto, on September 10, 1946, Mother Teresa heard Jesus calling to her distinctly and clearly. She would later describe it as "a call within a call" since she was already a nun. Jesus was asking her to start a new religious congregation that would take care of the poorest of the poor, starting in Calcutta. "Come, come, carry Me into the holes of the poor. Come, be My light," Jesus instructed. She answered, "Yes." That was the very beginning of the Missionaries of Charity congregation.

As a Loretto Sister, in the founding of the Missionaries of Charity, and every day left to her, Mother Teresa fully embraced the Gospel message of Matthew in which we learn explicit and essential instructions from Jesus with regard to how we are to live our lives. At the end of our lives we will be judged by how we have loved and served others. Jesus promises a heavenly reward to the faithful, but is unmistakably straightforward about what will happen to those who have not lived holy lives, serving the poor. Our Lord and Savior said they will be cast into the fires of hell. We should know that God does not want us in hell. He desires that each and every person he has created will enjoy eternal happiness in heaven with him forever. However, God has also given each of us the gift of free will. We choose whether or not we will be good or evil, and whether or not we will follow the Commandments. It's unlikely that anyone would choose evil from the start. But the evil allurements of the world, which are instigated by the devil, whose job it is to snatch souls to hell, can tempt us to fall into evil. If we are not prayerful and vigilant, we can easily become seduced by the false promises of the modern world and eventually turn our backs on God. That is why it is so very important to surround ourselves with like-minded faithful people who can help us to stay on the straight and narrow path that leads to eternal life.

As mentioned earlier, Mother Teresa lived her life and vocation to satiate the thirst of Jesus on the Cross. She accomplished this through her many prayers and through her loving hands as she ministered to the sick and suffering. Our Lord's words, "Just as you did it to one of the least of these who are members of the family, you did it to me" (Matt. 25:40) were etched on Mother Teresa's heart as she lived this message wholeheartedly. She firmly believed that she was serving Jesus in every single person to whom she ministered, and that Jesus lived in her as well. She was a Catholic nun and called by God to service, but we too have a vocation; we too are called to love and serve.

How do we serve Jesus in others, especially the "least"?

Mother Teresa's loving prayerful actions teach us to follow her example. She explained that prayer is imperative to do the work. She taught simply. Holding up her hand, she counted down on her five fingers: "You-did-it-to-Me!" referring to the words in the Gospel of Matthew, "Truly I tell you, just as you did it to one of the least of these who are members of the family, you did it to me" (Matt. 25:40). Her life was a living testament to our Lord's directives to take care of the needy, the naked, the lonely, the poor, the small and insignificant, the most in need. This saint of the gutters changed the world with Christ's love because of her wholehearted "Yes!" to his will, whatever it would be and no matter how hard it was to do. God was always with her even when he seemed distant.

She talked about how Jesus put his love into action. "His love in action for us was the crucifixion," she reflected. She said that she and the Sisters needed to receive Jesus in the Eucharist at Mass each morning in order to have the strength to then take care of the broken bodies of the poor throughout the day. "That gives us the strength and the courage and the joy and the love to touch Him, to love Him, to serve Him. Without Him, we couldn't do it. With Him, we can do all things."

How do each of us serve Jesus in "the least"? For parents, each time you wash your child's face, tie a shoe, feed your babies in the night, bring peace to siblings, provide nutritious meals, or rescue your children from an ungodly culture, you are accomplishing much more than meets the eye when you strive to do it with Christ's love. You are certainly serving Jesus in the other. This goes for anyone in any state of life, whether religious or lay. We need to reach out with Christ's love and serve Jesus in those in need in our homes, neighborhoods, workplaces, and communities, and in the strangers we meet.

reflect

The words of Jesus in Matthew's Gospel thoroughly strengthened the petite nun as she went about serving the least. "Jesus said, 'Come, you who are blessed by my Father, inherit the kingdom prepared for you from the foundation of the world; for I was hungry and you gave me food, I was thirsty and you gave me something to drink, I was a stranger and you welcomed me, I was naked and you gave me clothing, I was sick and you took care of me, I was in prison and you visited me'" (Matt. 25:34–36). These words should be etched upon our hearts. Mother Teresa's holy life of serving the poor and needy edifies and inspires us. We can ask ourselves a few questions.

Do I welcome Jesus in the stranger? Do I welcome him in my family members? Keeping in mind that Mother Teresa believed that "love begins at home," do you pray and take action to care for needs in your family and in those around that you are able to help? Might there be some grudge or misunderstanding that needs to be taken to God in prayer and possibly a loving intervention of sorts with the people involved? What do you do and not do to Jesus? Ponder that. I think it is wise to also ponder the fact that Mother Teresa was just one person, and yet, by God's grace and her wholehearted surrender to his will, she was able to accomplish incredible things. What will your own "yes" to God accomplish? Now, pray the novena prayer.

Novena
prayer

St. Teresa of Calcutta, please hear my prayer. You are a faithful and devoted servant of our Lord and of his poor—those you called "The poorest of the poor," those in the greatest need, and those for whom our Lord instructs us to serve, saying, "Whatever you do to the least of my brothers you do to me." Through your life of holy service, you demonstrated the joy of loving and taught us the greatness and dignity of every human being, from conception to natural death. Your continual walk in faith to serve those in need even as you were stricken with hardship and darkness floods my soul with great hope. Please, dear Saint of the Gutters, help me in my present need by presenting my prayer petition before the throne of God.

[Here, mention your request.]

Please also intercede for me so that I may have the strength and courage to give my own personal "yes" each day and that I will come closer to our divine Lord Jesus Christ, ultimately joining you one day in praising him forever in heaven.

Amen.

five

Love Hurts

" I looked for compassion, but there was none,
for comforters, but found none."
—Psalm 69

True love often hurts, as Mother Teresa has often pointed out. Love is not always warm and fuzzy. Most of the time, it's not. Love requires sacrifice and effort on our part. When we have occasion to push through our comfort zones to love with a sacrificial love, we may find that it is utterly transforming. Mother Teresa said, "True love causes pain. Jesus, to give us the proof of His love, died on the cross. A mother, to give birth to her baby, has to suffer. If you really love one another, you will not be able to avoid making sacrifices." Mother Teresa knew that our sacrificial love can be redemptive. St. Faustina also knew well of loving until it "hurts." For instance, she said doing penance for her sister Wanda cost her a lot, possibly more than other sacrifices and sufferings she had endured. St. Faustina's suffering lovingly offered to God helped her sister.

How can we love until it hurts? Mother Teresa tells us how. "You must love with your time, your hands, and your hearts. You need to share all that you have." She shared some poignant stories about sacrificial love. She said one time there was trouble getting sugar into Calcutta. A little four-year-old Hindu boy showed up at the convent one day with a cup of sugar as a gift. He said he had been going without sugar for a few days and wanted to donate sugar to be used for the poor. Mother found the boy's gesture and gift to be lovely. She said, "That little boy loved to the point of sacrificing."

On another occasion, she was touched by observing a mother's sacrificial love for her neighbors. This began one evening when a man showed up at the convent door to alert Mother Teresa of a starving Hindu family with eight children. Mother quickly gathered some rice she had planned to use for supper and went off with the gentleman in search of the family. She recalled, "I could see the spectre of hunger drawn on the faces of the little children when we found the family. They looked like human skeletons." We can imagine the pain she felt in her heart. Mother Teresa joyfully handed over the rice. But, before they could sit down to eat, the mother of the house divided the portion in half and excused herself quickly to exit their abode. Mother Teresa wondered where she was going and immediately asked upon her return. The Hindu mother had gone next door to deliver half of the gift of rice to her hungry Muslim neighbors who also had a large, starving family. Mother Teresa smiled. She was so happy. She recalled, "What struck me was that she knew, and because she knew she gave until it hurt. That is something beautiful. That is love in action! That woman shared with great sacrifice."

How did she love sacrificially?

Mother Teresa's work with the poor was all about sacrificial love. Yes, she wholeheartedly loved her Lord and wanted to please him by doing his will and bringing many souls to him. But doing the loving and many times strenuous work required sacrifice. She rose before the sun every morning to pray and look over her congregation. She stuck with a schedule, put in place to get a lot accomplished—both in the hearts and souls of the sisters through their prayer lives, as well as for the lonely, sick, and suffering that they served. Being obedient to the schedule is one form of sacrificial love. Showing up at the chapel when the bell rings for prayer when you don't feel like it is an act of love. Pulling maggots out of a person left for dead in the gutter requires heroic and sacrificial love. All works of authentic love are for a Divine purpose. Striving to serve Jesus in the ones who contradict you, who spit on you, and who criticize you is also sacrificial love which can sometimes hurt one's heart. God gives us the grace to choose the high road and to respond with his love—always.

At one point, Mother Teresa disclosed that leaving the Loretto convent to begin her work in Calcutta was the biggest sacrifice of her life. She left the happiness of teaching her students and her family behind to follow God's call to her. She said, "The first step towards the slum is over. It cost a very good deal, but I am grateful to God for giving the grace to do it and also for showing me how very weak I am." We can't picture Mother Teresa as being "weak" as she says. We can be certain that it was in her humility that she said that. She was actually a powerhouse of faith, hope, and love—she was a do-er! Yet, she felt that God revealed her weakness to her in her feelings about leaving the comfort and familiarity of Loretto to cross over the threshold to the slums of Calcutta.

Still, what did Mother Teresa do when faced with the pain of leaving her family, her convent, and her joyful work? She immediately followed what she knew was our Lord's holy call to her heart to start the Missionaries of Charity and to minister to the "unwanted" and "forgotten" in Calcutta. This nun relied on prayer and God's grace through the sacraments to give her strength to make that major change. That took patience and perseverance. Her loving heart had to hurt to wholeheartedly embrace the will of God. That is real love. Walking forward in faith, with surrender and resignation, amid uncertainty, is sacrificial love.

How can we do it?

One time a man asked Mother Teresa what could be done to eliminate the poverty in Calcutta. She told him, "We need to learn to share with the poor." Along those lines, Mother Teresa said, "We cannot share unless our lives are full of God's love and our hearts are pure." We need prayer and the sacraments.

She explained, "As Jesus said, 'Blessed are the poor of heart, for they shall see God.'" She said, "Unless we are able to see God in our neighbor, it will be very hard for us to love." Again, she reminds us of where our love needs to begin. "Since love begins at home, let's love each other at home. Jesus said, 'Love one another as I have loved you.'" She underscored once again, "He loved until it hurt."

Mother Teresa discovered such beauty in being in love with Jesus and following his holy will. She expressed, "Jesus' love is so overwhelming that you and I can love Him and find life." Further, she explained how to love him and serve him with that kind of amazing sacrificial love: "We can love Jesus in the hungry, the naked, and the destitute who are dying." With what strength? She said: "We can love Him because our prayer gives us the faith we need to be able to love. If you love, you will be willing to serve.

And you will find Jesus in the distressing disguise of the poor." Very powerful words to take to our hearts.

reflect

In one of her letters to me, Mother Teresa asked me to "Be the one." She was referring to the verse above, beginning this day of our novena: "I looked for compassion, but there was none, for comforters, but found none" (Psalm 69). She told me that Jesus said he looked for one to comfort him but found none. She reminded me that he experienced deep loneliness in the Garden and on the Cross.

Mother Teresa encourages us all to "be the one." More likely than not, we won't be pulling maggots out of anyone anytime soon. But, what about the love we can show in our gentle smile at someone who is mean to us, or in the time we give to someone who needs to vent, or in being present to our family members, our neighbors, our co-workers when we are exhausted, and in showing love to a complete stranger when it is difficult to do so. Opportunities unfold for us to love sacrificially every day. Take time to ponder your own life and how God might be calling you to love more sacrificially. Strive to "be the one" to comfort Jesus through your prayers and good works. Now, pray the novena prayer.

Novena
prayer

St. Teresa of Calcutta, please hear my prayer. You are a faithful and devoted servant of our Lord and of his poor—those you called "The poorest of the poor," those in the greatest need, and those for whom our Lord instructs us to serve, saying, "Whatever you do to the least of my brothers you do to me." Through your life of holy service, you demonstrated the joy of loving and taught us the greatness and dignity of every human being, from conception to natural death. Your continual walk in faith to serve those in need even as you were stricken with hardship and darkness floods my soul with great hope. Please, dear Saint of the Gutters, help me in my present need by presenting my prayer petition before the throne of God.

[Here, mention your request.]

Please also intercede for me so that I may have the strength and courage to give my own personal "yes" each day and that I will come closer to our divine Lord Jesus Christ, ultimately joining you one day in praising him forever in heaven.

Amen.

six

Joy Is a Net of Love

> " Cheerfulness is a sign of a generous
> and mortified person who forgetting all things,
> even herself, tries to please God
> in all she does for souls."
> —Mother Teresa

Joy is a fruit of the Holy Spirit. It should grow in our soul, stemming from the gifts of the Holy Spirit. The Catechism instructs, "The *fruits* of the Spirit are perfections that the Holy Spirit forms in us as the first fruits of eternal glory. The tradition of the Church lists twelve of them: 'charity, joy, peace, patience, kindness, goodness, generosity, gentleness, faithfulness, modesty, self-control, chastity' (CCC 1832). We also read about joy in Galatians: 'By contrast, the fruit of the Spirit is love, joy, peace, patience, kindness, generosity, faithfulness, gentleness, and self-control. There is no law against such things' (Galatians, 5:22-23)."

Joy is powerful! Mother Teresa often preached about the importance of possessing joy in our hearts. She said, "Joy is prayer. Joy is strength. Joy is love. Joy is a net of love by which you can catch souls." She mentioned joy in all of her letters to me. Before she signed off, she usually wrote, "Keep the joy of loving Jesus always in your heart and share this joy with others."

I witnessed great joy radiating from Mother Teresa's eyes and could truly feel it come from her heart whenever I was near her and whenever I read what she wrote. Joy was very important to this saint. In speaking about the need to be joyful when ministering to the needy, she said, "If we went to them with a sad face, we would only make them much more depressed." For this reason, Mother Teresa told her sisters that they needed joy in their hearts, otherwise they should just pack up and go home. That might seem harsh, but Mother Teresa taught a foundational lesson—joy is essential to their work with the poor. She said, "If one of my sisters is not in at least a serene mood, I do not allow her to go visit the poor. The poor already have so many reasons to feel sad; how could we take them the affliction of our own personal bad moods?" Along the same lines, she explained, "Our poor people suffer much, and unless we go with joy we cannot help them. We will make them more miserable."

Mother Teresa delighted in smiles—especially on her sisters' faces and upon seeing the ones that spread across the faces of those they served. She once told the story of a woman she found dying in the streets of Calcutta. She took her in and got her into a bed, though she knew there wasn't anything she could do for her medically. The woman was beyond that. As soon as she was tucked into bed, Mother Teresa held her hand lovingly. The woman opened her eyes to look straight at Mother. A peaceful smile lit up her face and she spoke softly, "Thank you." The woman closed her eyes and died. Mother Teresa never forgot that moment—that smile.

Mother Teresa expressed, "A joyful Sister is like: the sunshine of God's love, the Hope of eternal happiness, the Flame of burning love." As well, she asserted, "A Sister filled with joy preaches without preaching. Joy is a need and a power for us even physically, for it makes us always ready to go about doing good. The joy of the Lord is our strength." The Holy Spirit's fruit of joy was so important to Mother Teresa that she mentioned it in the Missionaries of Charity Constitution, which stipulates, "A spirit of joy should permeate the daily life of the novitiate and the novices should be encouraged to regard the communicating of this joy as a necessary part of their apostolate" (No. 203).

That same radiant joy of the Missionaries of Charity caught the eye of a young woman who became very attracted to their vocation after volunteering for a short while in Calcutta. That young woman expressed her observations: "I came to Calcutta as a tourist to work for Mother Teresa's poor for a few months. When I saw the happiness and joy of the Sisters doing this work, I felt attracted to this kind of life." She explained, "In my country I had never thought of becoming a nun. Those I had met looked gloomy: they were plagued with problems, worries, anxieties." This young woman surmised, "They thought something had gone wrong with the world, and they were not able to correct it." The thought of becoming a nun had never crossed her mind until after she spent some time with the Missionaries of Charity. She said, "But here the Sisters have no problems, no anxieties. They allow God to lead them. This gives them happiness and joy." Undoubtedly, God was speaking to this young woman's heart through their joy. The woman knew what she had to do and went straight to it. She wrote to her parents to inform that she had decided to join the Missionaries of Charity. She said, "Now I am a postulant."

Joy is love and a characteristic mark of a Christian

Mother Teresa told her sisters, "Joy is love, the normal result of a heart burning with love. Our lamp will be burning with sacrifices made out of love if we have joy. Then the Bridegroom will say, 'Come and possess the Kingdom prepared for you.'" She explained, "It is a joyful Sister who gives most. Everyone loves the one who gives with joy and so does God." She added, "Don't we always turn to someone who will give happily and without grumbling?" Mother Teresa deeply desired that they would radiate a contagious and magnetic joy.

We can do the same, where we are. Mother said, "In Bethlehem, joy filled everyone: the shepherds, the angels, the Kings, Joseph, and Mary. Joy was also the characteristic mark of the first Christians." During early Christian persecutions, Mother Teresa explained, "People used to look for those who had this joy radiating on their faces. By that joy, they knew who the Christians were and thus they persecuted them." Then she came to the great apostle of joy. She said, "St Paul, whom we are trying to imitate in our zeal, was an apostle of joy. He urged the early Christians to rejoice in the Lord always." She said, "Paul's whole life can be summed up in one sentence, 'I belong to Christ.' Nothing can separate me from the Love of Christ, neither suffering nor persecution nor anything. 'I live, now it is no longer I who live but it is Christ who lives in me.' That is why St. Paul was so full of joy," she explained.

Mother Teresa believed that we should also show our joy to God—to be joyful toward him. We should be grateful for all he gives us. She said, "The best way to show our gratitude to God and the people is to accept everything with joy." She encourages us, saying: "Never let anything so fill you with sorrow as to make you forget the joy of the Risen Christ." The hero for the poorest of the poor urges us to be joyful people. She pointed out, "We all long for Heaven where God is, but we have it in our power to be in Heaven with him right now, to be happy with him at this very moment." We should endeavor to "be in heaven" with him now and be that radiant joy in a world filled with pain and sorrow.

reflect

Are you a joyful person? If not, why not? Yes, we live in a world that does not support our Christianity. Yes, we face a myriad of challenges and contradictions that can cause us to fear or become saddened. We might feel sorrowful over a loss, struggle, or misunderstanding. Yet, joy can reside in our hearts even if we have sorrow and pain. It is a holy joy that exists knowing there is a promise of eternal life that follows this one. Mother Teresa reminds us that joy is very important and that a joyful person can attract souls to God. Ponder your life and strive to make necessary changes that will allow the Holy

Spirit's fruit of joy grow in your heart. Start today by praying to the Holy Spirit to ask for joy to enter your heart. Talk to God throughout your day—tell him how you feel. Ask him to lift your burdens or give you the grace to accept them with a smile and offer them back to him for the conversion of sinners. As Mother Teresa has suggested, smile at least five times a day! Try that. Now, pray the novena prayer.

Novena
prayer

St. Teresa of Calcutta, please hear my prayer. You are a faithful and devoted servant of our Lord and of his poor—those you called "The poorest of the poor," those in the greatest need, and those for whom our Lord instructs us to serve, saying, "Whatever you do to the least of my brothers you do to me." Through your life of holy service, you demonstrated the joy of loving and taught us the greatness and dignity of every human being, from conception to natural death. Your continual walk in faith to serve those in need even as you were stricken with hardship and darkness floods my soul with great hope. Please, dear Saint of the Gutters, help me in my present need by presenting my prayer petition before the throne of God.

[Here, mention your request.]

Please also intercede for me so that I may have the strength and courage to give my own personal "yes" each day and that I will come closer to our divine Lord Jesus Christ, ultimately joining you one day in praising him forever in heaven.

Amen.

seven

Silence, Prayer, and Holiness

" In the silence of the heart, God speaks. "
—Mother Teresa

Mother Teresa often said that God is a friend of silence. She gave me a little yellow card that she called her "business card." It read, "The fruit of Silence is Prayer. The fruit of Prayer is Faith. The fruit of Faith is Love. The fruit of Love is Service. The fruit of Service is Peace." We could stop right here and take the time to reflect upon those concise statements, pondering how one fruit leads to the other. But it all starts with silence. If we really meditate on those poignant statements we could come to a better understanding of how Mother Teresa's mind and heart ticked. She absolutely knew that silence is essential in the spiritual life.

Mother once extolled, "The first requirement for prayer is silence. People of prayer are people of silence." She also said, "Mary can teach us silence—how to keep all things in our hearts as she did, to pray in the silence of our hearts." We know without doubt that it is awfully difficult to find silence in our noisy and convoluted world. Yet it is necessary to discover the silence somehow mysteriously woven into our busy days. We will get to that.

People often asked her what her amazing secret was. How did she do all that she accomplished? She simply said, "I pray." That was her big secret to sanctity. She prayed. Prayer is what enabled her to make those great strides (on those very short legs!) to found the Missionaries of Charity congregation, which serves the poor and unwanted all over the world.

Now, what about the rest of us? I'm not going to simply say: Go out and be Mother Teresa. As if we could! But, we might ask: How can we strive to pray like Mother Teresa? She teaches us precisely how.

"If we really want to pray, we must first learn to listen: for in the silence of the heart God speaks. And to be able to see that silence, to be able to hear God, we need a clean heart," she said. What do we do in the silence that we hope to discover? We listen. Mother said, "Let us listen to God, to what He has to say. We cannot speak unless we have listened, unless we have made our connection with God." Further, she instructs, "From the fullness of the heart, the mouth will speak, the mind will think." So, we must find silence in which to pray. Let us also remember that she said we need a "clean heart." That means that we should be in the state of grace. We insult God when we expect so many things from him in prayer, yet we have turned our backs on him and have broken the Commandments or refuse to go to Confession.

Finding Silence, Becoming Holy

We are familiar with the now-famous sentiment of St. Augustine, "Our hearts are restless until they rest in you." We know that prayer is necessary for spiritual survival. Mother Teresa admitted that she wouldn't be able to do even a half-hour of work without prayer. Prayer and the sacraments were necessary for her. They fueled her heart so that she could continue to walk in faith and lead her sisters and the poor they served closer and closer to Heaven. Prayer and Mother's relationship with Jesus were the cement in the foundation of her spiritual life.

This humble nun urges us to strive, too, for silence so we can get our prayers right. It is not impossible to find the important silence that is needed for prayer, though we know how busy and noisy each day can be. It is up to us to make time for silence by seeking it out. As well, we need to curb our chatty natures and allow God to do at least some of the talking. A conversation requires two. It should never be one-sided. Mother Teresa tells us very simply, "Prayer is simply talking to God. He speaks to us, we listen. We speak to Him, He listens. A two-way process: speaking and listening." God will indeed speak to our hearts. Let's make sure we are listening.

Mother Teresa often said we are all called to holiness—each of us in our own state of life. She said that holiness is not reserved for a few, but a simple duty for each one of us. She said, "To become holy we need humility and prayer." We discussed humility earlier in this novena. Mother Teresa reminds us, "Jesus taught us how to pray, and he also told us to learn from him to be meek and humble of heart." Yet, Mother Teresa boldly instructs, "Neither of these can we do unless we know what is silence." Silence is that important. She explained, "Both humility and prayer grow from an ear, mind, and tongue that have lived in silence with God, for in the silence of the heart God speaks."

Some called her a "true force of nature." She was certainly countercultural in what she taught and in how she lived. She urged us to seek silence and told people in big cities to look hard for silence, because that is "where everything moves so fast." Then, she even did something that seems contradictory. We might envision that nuns living in a serene environment could pray well contemplatively. But what did Mother Teresa do? She said, "I decided to open our first home for contemplative sisters (whose vocation is to pray most of the day) in New York instead of the Himalayas: I felt silence and contemplation were needed more in the cities of the world." I have visited that New York City convent, and it is right at the heart of the noise. If the sisters there can find silence in which to immerse their hearts in prayer, we can also discover it right where we are.

Another Kind of Silence

There's another kind of silence, as well. That is the silence of God. At times throughout the spiritual life, a person might experience a "dark night." This term was most likely first penned by St. John of the Cross, who wrote about the dark night and how a soul is purged and burnished in God's love during this process. At times the period of darkness can feel utterly debilitating. We know that Mother Teresa endured an extremely long dark night, which came over her soon after she crossed the threshold into the slums of Calcutta. She no longer received wonderful consoling locutions from Jesus and Mary and peaceful feelings when receiving the sacraments. No, she needed to rely solely on faith. She did not have a crisis of faith, as some commentators described it, making headlines when we first learned about this part of her life years ago. If that were true, Mother wouldn't have continued to walk in faith despite the feelings of abandonment and desolation she experienced in her soul.

This may sound contradictory, but our Lord often allows those he loves and whom he is calling to be great saints to experience some of the things he went through. At times, it might be through enduring a dark night. Sometimes, it might be through trials and tribulations. Whatever the challenge, we need to continue to pray and ask God for all the graces necessary to get to the other side of the trials. As well, we can ask God to use our suffering for his glory and the good of others. It's that old-fashioned phrase of "offering it up," put into action.

St. Teresa of Avila, a sixteenth-century Carmelite nun, often spoke candidly and often with humor. At one point when she was on a dangerous journey during stormy weather, she ended up almost carried away by strong currents of a stream. The Lord rescued her from the rushing current, and St. Teresa cried out, "Oh, my Lord! When will You stop scattering obstacles in our path?" Jesus said to her, "Do not complain, daughter, for that is the way I always treat My friends." We can certainly smile, yet we should take note that difficulties are guaranteed along the straight and narrow path that leads to heaven. God was not silent in this case, but I think we can grasp the point here.

Pope Emeritus Benedict XVI once commented on the silence of God in Mother Teresa's life. "All believers know about the silence of God," he said. Then he pointed out, "Even Mother Teresa, with all her charity and force of faith, suffered from the silence of God." So, we should expect that God will be silent at times, and we should strive to find silence, which is so necessary for prayer.

reflect

Ponder your prayer life. Do you make enough time for God? We certainly need to take the time to listen to God speaking to our hearts. We won't be able to hear him with a cluttered mind and heart and by immersing ourselves in endless noise through our involvement in too much activity and media. We need to search our hearts and see what might get in the way of our conversations with God, as well as to carve out time for prayer.

Mother Teresa tells us that every one of us is called to a life of holiness. The secret to holiness lies in the state of our souls, our prayer lives, and our faithfulness to our duties. God will indeed speak to our contrite and humble hearts. Let's be sure to listen. Let's ask Mother Mary to help us to be more quiet and to find silence for prayer. Now, pray the novena prayer.

Novena
prayer

St. Teresa of Calcutta, please hear my prayer. You are a faithful and devoted servant of our Lord and of his poor—those you called "The poorest of the poor," those in the greatest need, and those for whom our Lord instructs us to serve, saying, "Whatever you do to the least of my brothers you do to me." Through your life of holy service, you demonstrated the joy of loving and taught us the greatness and dignity of every human being, from conception to natural death. Your continual walk in faith to serve those in need even as you were stricken with hardship and darkness floods my soul with great hope. Please, dear Saint of the Gutters, help me in my present need by presenting my prayer petition before the throne of God.

[Here, mention your request.]

Please also intercede for me so that I may have the strength and courage to give my own personal "yes" each day and that I will come closer to our divine Lord Jesus Christ, ultimately joining you one day in praising him forever in heaven.

Amen.

eight

Love Begins at Home

" Love begins at home, and it is not how much
we do, but how much love we put in the action
that we do. It is to God Almighty—
how much we do it does not matter, because
He is infinite, but how much love we put in
that action. How much we do to Him
in the person that we are serving."
—Mother Teresa, Nobel Peace Prize speech

The faithful are called to spread the Gospel.
How is that accomplished? We read in the
Psalms, "The Gospel must be preached to all
nations" (Ps. 66, cf. Mk. 13:10). Yet, most times we
feel we lack the necessary time or energy to go out
and "preach" in whatever way that may be for each
of us. It's important to realize that though our Lord
calls us to evangelize and spread the Gospel, we
must do it according to our particular state of life.
Mother Teresa was famous for saying, "Love begins
at home." That is where we start our "preaching." That

is where we spread the Gospel—first within our own homes, which are our domestic churches; then we may broaden our reach. It would actually be wrong for us to go out and preach elsewhere or try to save the world and neglect our own family in the process.

Mother Teresa loved all people, but her heart went out to the defenseless. She once said about the babies she cared for, "These babies must not die uncared for and unloved because even a tiny baby can feel." My very first conversation with her was about family. When we met the first time in Washington DC at the Gift of Peace House, she told me that my children were very lucky to have a family. She was, you see, accustomed to rescuing discarded babies out of dustbins. These might have been babies whose leper parents could no longer care for them. I immediately told this fiery little nun dressed in a simple cotton sari that I was immensely blessed to have my children. Those twin sentiments began a beautiful conversation.

Mother Teresa encouraged the world to take care of their families, and not to fail in looking deep within our own families to make certain that their needs have been taken care of before we attempt to spread our love elsewhere. It is possible that there is someone in our family who is feeling neglected or starving for love (even though we are loving them). It could be something they are going through. We need to search our hearts. Mother didn't speak to audiences very often, since her life's work was in ministering to the poorest of the poor.

But, once in a while, she was asked to speak at various events or when receiving awards. In an address at the National Prayer Breakfast, among other subjects, including speaking out against abortion, Mother spoke about the family and the need to let love begin there. It was the start of the "Year of the Family," and she explained she was surprised that in the Western world so many young people are on drugs. She said she wanted to find out why. She reminded her audience, "Our children depend on us for everything—their health, their nutrition, their security, their coming to know and love God. For all of this, they look to us with trust, hope and expectation." She then went straight to the crux of the matter. "But often father and mother are so busy they have no time for their children, or perhaps they are not even married or have given up on their marriage. So their children go to the streets and get involved in drugs or other things." She said, "Love of the child . . . is where love and peace must begin." She explained that the absence of the parents and their lack of involvement are "the things that break peace."

Mother encouraged and challenged her audience: "I want you to find the poor here, right in your own home first. And begin love there. Be that good news to your own people first. And find out about your next-door neighbors. Do you know who they are?" We all need to reach out to our neighbors. We need to let our love spread around us, to those who are nearby.

One time, Mother Teresa sadly lamented how a woman had died in a New York City apartment and was already being eaten by rats before her body was found. This tireless hero for the poor was thoroughly upset that the woman's neighbors didn't even know she existed, and the woman was left to die alone. A pitiful woman that she had never met was for Mother a symbol of the great need all around us wherever we look.

reflect

We learn a very important lesson from Mother Teresa about making sure that we love those in our families first before running off to save the world. We need to take time with our families and get to know our neighbors and offer them Christ's love as well. The saint of the gutters said, "We must remember that love begins at home and we must also remember that the future of humanity passes through the family." In her speech, Mother Teresa was quoting St.

John Paul II who stated in his Apostolic Exhortation *Familiaris Consortio* that "the future of humanity passes by way of the family." He then implored "every person of good will" to "save and foster the values and requirements of the family" because the family is so important to humanity's future.

Ponder Mother Teresa's words today about love beginning at home, and pray the novena prayer.

Novena
prayer

St. Teresa of Calcutta, please hear my prayer. You are a faithful and devoted servant of our Lord and of his poor—those you called "The poorest of the poor," those in the greatest need, and those for whom our Lord instructs us to serve, saying, "Whatever you do to the least of my brothers you do to me." Through your life of holy service, you demonstrated the joy of loving and taught us the greatness and dignity of every human being, from conception to natural death. Your continual walk in faith to serve those in need even as you were stricken with hardship and darkness floods my soul with great hope. Please, dear Saint of the Gutters, help me in my present need by presenting my prayer petition before the throne of God.

[Here, mention your request.]

Please also intercede for me so that I may have the strength and courage to give my own personal "yes" each day and that I will come closer to our divine Lord Jesus Christ, ultimately joining you one day in praising him forever in heaven.

Amen.

nine

Be a Mother to Me

" Let us be all for Jesus through Mary."
—Mother Teresa

Mother Teresa wholeheartedly knew the power and passion in a mother's love. She never mothered a child biologically, but she spiritually mothered countless people all around the globe. She certainly mothered me.

Mother begged for all unwanted babies whose mothers contemplated abortion or who couldn't care for a child and said she'd care for them herself. She took them in, cared for them, and placed them for adoption in loving homes. She also taught us how to be "spiritual mothers" by opening our eyes and hearts to the needy around us whom we should "mother."

Mother teaches us that Mother Mary wants to be our mother, too, and will always lead us to her Son. We may fear that Mary is some unreachable saint of ages past, and because of this we fail to reach out to her as we should. But we need to remember that Jesus gifted us with his mother when he was dying on the Cross: "Here is your mother," he said. Jesus wants us to get close to her and call upon her often. Mary will always lead us closer to her Son, Jesus. After all, she said, "Do whatever he tells you," when a wedding party was without wine. She trusted her Son, who was also her Messiah. She left everything up to him, and she encourages us to do the same.

St. Teresa of Calcutta was humbly devoted to the Blessed Mother. In fact, Mary spoke to Mother Teresa through locutions during the same time period that Jesus was requesting that she found the new religious order that would serve the poorest of the poor.

A few years later, I was blessed to see Mother Teresa in action as well as at prayer when I visited her at her convents. So often the beads of her worn rosary made their way through Mother's tired fingers as she silently prayed the rosary, beseeching Mother Mary's help for the task at hand. When her hands were busy with the work, she prayed to the Blessed Mother from her heart. On one occasion, I was in her convent's chapel at a rare time when it was empty. In walked Mother Teresa. Imagine how my heart soared as she quietly knelt nearby, and by God's grace our hearts were mysteriously and lovingly joined in adoration of Jesus in the Blessed Sacrament. Mother Mary was no doubt present as well. She is always with her Son.

Mother Teresa encouraged others to get very close to Mary. We must do this if we want to see Jesus most clearly.

Mother Teresa said, "It is very, very important for us to have a deep love for our Lady. For she was the one who taught Jesus how to walk, how to pray, how to wash, how to do all the little things that make our human life so beautiful. She had to do them." Mother Teresa explained how she helps us: "And the same thing now—she will always be willing to help us and teach us how to be all for Jesus alone, how to love only Jesus, how to touch him and see him, to serve him in the distressing disguise." She said that cheerfulness and joy are Mary's strength.

Be a Mother to me now

At one point I was on complete bed rest with a high-risk pregnancy after my uterus hemorrhaged at ten weeks gestation. I had already lost three babies to miscarriage, and the doctor didn't think this baby was going to make it, either. I had to pray hard, follow doctor's orders to stay still, resign myself to God's will, and wait and see.

I got word to Mother Teresa and asked for her prayers. Mother told me to entrust my precarious pregnancy to the Blessed Mother. She sent me a blessed Miraculous Medal, which I still wear today. She told me, "Just put yourself in the hands of our Blessed Mother and let her take care of you. When you are sad or troubled just tell her so. She will prove herself a Mother to you. Pray often, 'Mary, Mother of Jesus, make me all right'; 'Mary, Mother of Jesus, be Mother to me now.'" Her words were comforting, and I followed her advice and prayed to Mary often. Thanks be to God, both baby and I survived that pregnancy and my "baby" is now twenty-seven years old! I believe that Mother Mary helped us immensely, and I named my daughter after her.

Mother Teresa often spoke about Mary's loving missionary visit to her cousin Elizabeth that we read about in Scripture (Lk. 1:39–45). Mother Teresa explained, "Mary was a true missionary because she was not afraid to be the handmaid of the Lord. She went in haste to put her beautiful humility into a living action of love, to do the handmaid's work for Elizabeth." Amazing things happened during this visit between the Mother of God with Jesus residing in her womb and St. Elizabeth with St. John the Baptist nestled in hers. Mother Teresa said, "We know what this humility obtained for the unborn child: he 'leapt with joy' in the womb of his mother—the first human being to recognize the coming of Christ; and then the mother of the Lord sang with joy, with gratitude, and praise."

Mother Teresa underscored the main virtue operating in Mary's heart. She explained, "The greatness of our Lady was in her humility. No wonder Jesus, who lived so close to her, seemed to be so anxious that we learn from him and from her but one lesson: to be meek and humble of heart." We too must strive to be meek and humble of heart. Humility is at the heart of every other virtue. Jesus needs our humble hearts to accomplish his will through us. His own humble, loving heart was formed under the heart of his Mother, Mary.

The Blessed Mother "will teach us her humility: though full of grace—yet only the handmaid of the Lord; though the mother of God—yet serving like a handmaid in the house of Elizabeth; though conceived Immaculate—she meets Jesus humiliated, carrying his cross, and near the cross she stands as one of us, as if she were a sinner needing redemption." This is what Mother Teresa teaches us. We must surrender to God's will. Mother Teresa instructs, "Like her [Mary], let us always accept the cross in whatever way it may come." Mary will certainly help us. Then, Mother Teresa offers this heartfelt prayer: "Humility of the heart of Mary, fill my heart. Teach me as you taught Jesus to be meek and humble of heart and so glorify our Father."

We can look to the Blessed Mother as an exemplary virtuous and loving example. We can also seek Mary's help throughout our super-packed days in the care of our families and households, feeling confident that Mary understands what parents are all about. For those who are not parents, we can be confident knowing that she knows our hearts and will help us to get to Heaven one day. Recall the wonderful selfless act of Mary who "ran in haste" to help her older cousin Elizabeth. We should strive and pray to emulate the beautiful virtues that Mary practiced. We, too, will be called to "run in haste" in various situations in life— in our own families, neighborhoods, workplaces, and communities. Our Lord calls us to possess loving hearts that seek to serve like his dear Mother Mary.

reflect

Mother Teresa gave me a prayer card that contained her heartfelt words in a prayer to Mary: "Mary, Mother of Jesus, give me Your heart so beautiful, so pure, so Immaculate, so full of love and humility that I may be able to receive Jesus in the Bread of Life, love Him as you loved Him and serve Him in the distressing disguise of the Poorest of the Poor." Take time to ponder Mother Teresa's words.

Recalling that cheerfulness and joy were Mary's strength, and that humility of heart sent Mother Mary to "run in haste" to help, let's never fear reaching out for help from Mother Mary. Do you need Mary's help, today? Consider someone else, too: Do you need to run in haste to anyone's aid, today?

Mary is so loving and kind. She was given to us as a gift by her Son, Jesus, and she wants to be a mother to us. Mother Teresa trusted her implicitly. So should we. "Mary, Mother of Jesus, be Mother to me now." Pray the novena prayer now.

Novena
prayer

St. Teresa of Calcutta, please hear my prayer. You are a faithful and devoted servant of our Lord and of his poor—those you called "The poorest of the poor," those in the greatest need, and those for whom our Lord instructs us to serve, saying, "Whatever you do to the least of my brothers you do to me." Through your life of holy service, you demonstrated the joy of loving and taught us the greatness and dignity of every human being, from conception to natural death. Your continual walk in faith to serve those in need even as you were stricken with hardship and darkness floods my soul with great hope. Please, dear Saint of the Gutters, help me in my present need by presenting my prayer petition before the throne of God.

[Here, mention your request.]

Please also intercede for me so that I may have the strength and courage to give my own personal "yes" each day and that I will come closer to our divine Lord Jesus Christ, ultimately joining you one day in praising him forever in heaven.

Amen.

about the author

Donna-Marie Cooper O'Boyle is a Catholic wife, mother of five children, a grandmother, and an award-winning and best-selling author and journalist, TV host, international speaker, and pilgrimage and retreat leader. She is the EWTN television host of *Everyday Blessings for Catholic Moms, Catholic Mom's Cafe,* and *Feeding Your Family's Soul,* which she created to teach, encourage, and inspire Catholic families. Her love of children teaching the Faith has motivated her as a catechist for nearly thirty years. She is also an extraordinary Eucharistic minister at her parish. Donna-Marie was noted as one of the Top Ten Most Fascinating Catholics in 2009 by *Faith & Family Live.* She enjoyed a decade-long friendship with Mother Teresa of Calcutta and became a Lay Missionary of Charity. For many years her spiritual director was Servant of God John A. Hardon, SJ, who also served as one of Mother Teresa's spiritual directors.

Donna-Marie is the author of thirty books on faith and family, including *Feeding Your Family's Soul, The Miraculous Medal, Angels for Kids,* and her memoir, *The Kiss of Jesus: How Mother Teresa and the Saints Helped Me to Discover the Beauty of the Cross.* She has been profiled on many television shows, including Fox News, *Rome Reports, Vatican Insider, Women of Grace,*

Sunday Night Prime, *EWTN Live*, *At Home with Jim and Joy*, *The Journey Home*, and *Faith & Culture* on EWTN. Donna-Marie lives with her family in beautiful rural New England, and she lectures throughout the world on topics relating to Catholic and Christian women, faith, and families, the saints, and her friend Mother Teresa. She can be reached at her websites: www.donnacooperoboyle.com and www.feedingyourfamilyssoul.com, where you can learn more about Donna-Marie's books, ministry, and pilgrimages, and where she also maintains blogs.

notes

PAGE

7 *The biggest disease today:* Catholic News Service,
September 4, 2016: http://www.catholicnews.com
/services/englishnews/2016/mother-teresa-do-small
-things-with-great-love.cfm

10 *All for Jesus. You see, I've always seen things in this light:*
http://www.asianews.it/news-en/Mother-Teresa,-the
-war-in-Lebanon-and-the-rescue-of-100-orphans-and
-children-with-disabilities-38470.html

11 *The biggest disease today is not leprosy or tuberculosis:*
Catholic News Service: http://www.catholicnews.com
/services/englishnews/2016/mother-teresa-do-small
-things-with-great-love.cfm

14 *Do ordinary things with extraordinary love: National
Catholic Register,* August 26, 2010: http://www.ncregister
.com/daily-news/do-ordinary-things-with
-extraordinary-love

15 *The greatest evil is the lack of love and charity:* Catholic
News Service: http://www.catholicnews.com/services
/englishnews/2016/mother-teresa-do-small-things-with
-great-love.cfm

16 *Peace begins with a smile:* Donna-Marie Cooper O'Boyle,
Bringing Lent Home with Mother Teresa, 2nd Edn. (Notre
Dame, IN: Ave Maria Press, 2012), "Tuesday, Fifth Week
of Lent," n.p.

18 *Let us keep very small:* Donna-Marie Cooper O'Boyle,
Catholic Wisdom for A Mother's Heart (Brewster, MA:
Paraclete Press, 2018), 150.

22 *Certainly for water:* http://w2.vatican.va/content
/francesco/en/speeches/2016/september/documents
/papa-francesco_20160920_assisi-preghiera-pace.html

23 *At this most difficult time He proclaimed:* August 9, 1992, Mother Teresa's instructions to the MC Sisters, in Joseph Langford, *Mother Teresa's Secret Fire* (Huntington, IN: Our Sunday Visitor, 2008), n.p.

24 *When He was dying on the Cross:* Mother Teresa's address to the National Prayer Breakfast, Feb. 3, 1994, http://www.ewtn.com/new_library/breakfast.htm

25 *Why does Jesus say 'I Thirst':* Joseph Langford, *Mother Teresa's Secret Fire*, 56.

27n1 *Love is not words:* Donna-Marie Cooper O'Boyle, *By Dawn's Early Light* (Bedford, NH: Sophia Institute Press, 2018), 177.

27n2 *wanted to give God something very beautiful:* Mother Teresa to Father Picachy, April 4, 1960, in Teresa of Calcutta, *Come Be My Light* (New York: Image, 2009), 29.

28 *Come, come, carry Me:* Teresa of Calcutta, *Come Be My Light*, 44, see also 98.

30 *His love in action for us was the crucifixion:* Ann Petrie and Jeanette Petrie, documentary film *Mother Teresa* (New York: Petrie Productions, 1986), quoted in Susan Conroy, *Mother Teresa's Lessons of Love and Secrets of Sanctity* (Notre Dame, IN: Our Sunday Visitor, 2003), n.p.

34 *True love causes pain: Mother Teresa: In My Own Words*, compiled by Jose Luis Gonzalez-Balado (Liguori, MO: Liguori, 2004), 35.

35n1 *You must love with your time: One Heart Full of Love: Mother Teresa*, edited by Jose Luis Gonzalez-Balado, (Ann Arbor, MI: Servant, 1988), 8.

35n2 *That little boy loved:* Ibid, 9.

36 *What struck me was that she knew:* Ibid, 10.

37 *The first step towards the slum is over:* Teresa of Calcutta, *Come Be My Light*, 124.

38 *Jesus' love is so overwhelming: One Heart Full of Love: Mother Teresa*, 42, 43.

42n1 *Joy is prayer:* Edward Joly, *Mother Teresa: Messenger of God's Love* (Staten Island, NY: St Paul's, 2004), 54.

42n2 *If we went to them with a sad face:* Malcom Muggeridge, *Something Beautiful for God* (New York: HarperOne, 2003), 98.

42n3 *If one of my sisters is not in at least a serene mood:* Mother Teresa, *A Life For God: Mother Teresa Treasury* (Grand Rapids, MI: Zondervan, 1996), 73.

42n4 *Our poor people suffer much:* Angelo Devananda, *Mother Teresa: Contemplative at the Heart of the World* (Ann Arbor, MI: Servant, 1985), 118.

43n1 *A joyful Sister is like:* Joly, *Mother Teresa: Messenger of God's Love,* 56.

43n2 *A Sister filled with joy:* Devananda, *Mother Teresa: Contemplative at the Heart of the World,* 61.

44n1 *I came to Calcutta as a tourist:* Joly, *Mother Teresa: Messenger of God's Love,* 56.

44n2 *Joy is love:* Devananda, *Mother Teresa: Contemplative at the Heart of the World,* 63.

45 *The best way to show our gratitude:* Ibid, 55.

49n1 *The first requirement for prayer is silence:* Mother Teresa: In My Own Words, 8.

49n2 *Mary can teach us silence:* Mother Teresa, *Love: A Fruit always in Season,* Dorothy S. Hunt, ed., (San Francisco: Ignatius, 1987), 154.

50n1 *If we really want to pray:* Mother Teresa: The Joy in Loving, Jaya Chaliha and Edward Le Joly, compilers (New York: Viking, 1997), March 27.

50n2 *Prayer is simply talking to God:* Ibid, May 4.

51 *To become holy we need humility and prayer:* Mother Teresa and Angelo Devananda, *Jesus, The Word to Be Spoken: Prayers and Meditations for Every Day of the Year,* Angelo D. Scolozzi, compiler (Ann Arbor, MI: Servant, 1999), June 30.

52 *I decided to open our first home:* Mother Teresa, *A Simple Path,* Lucinda Vardey, compiler (New York: Ballantine, 1995), 7.

54n1 *Oh, my Lord!:* Alice Lady Love, *The Life of Saint Teresa* (London: Herbert & Daniel, 1912), alt.

54n2 *All believers know about the silence of God:* https://www .reuters.com/article/us-pope-teresa/pope-says-mother -teresa-felt-gods-silence-idUSL0126531020070901

57 *Love begins at home:* From Nobel Lectures, Peace 1971–1980, Editor-in-Charge Tore Frängsmyr, Editor Irwin Abrams (Singapore: World Scientific Publishing Co., 1997, quoted in https://www.nobelprize.org/ nobel_prizes/peace/laureates/1979/teresa-lecture. html#footnote1

58 *These babies must not die uncared for:* Spink, *Mother Teresa*, 61.

59 *I want you to find the poor here:* Mother Teresa's address to the National Prayer Breakfast, Feb. 3, 1994, http://www .ewtn.com/new_library/breakfast.htm

60 *We must remember that love begins at home:* From the Nobel speech noted above.

61n1 *the future of humanity passes by way of the family:* Familiaris Consortio, # 86, http://w2.vatican.va/content /john-paul-ii/en/apost_exhortations/documents/hf_jp -ii_exh_19811122_familiaris-consortio.html

61n2 *every person of good will:* https://www.osv.com /OSVNewsweekly/Story/TabId/2672/ArtMID/13567 /ArticleID/6588/Motherly-wisdom-from-Blessed-Teresa .aspx

65 *It is very, very important for us:* Mother Teresa and Angelo Devananda, *Jesus, The Word to be Spoken*, May 1.

66n1 *Mary was a true missionary:* Ibid., May 2.

66n2 *The greatness of our Lady was in her humility:* Ibid., May 3.

67 *will teach us her humility:* Ibid., May 5.

about Paraclete Press

Who We Are

As the publishing arm of the Community of Jesus, Paraclete Press presents a full expression of Christian belief and practice—from Catholic to Evangelical, from Protestant to Orthodox, reflecting the ecumenical charism of the Community and its dedication to sacred music, the fine arts, and the written word. We publish books, recordings, sheet music, and video/DVDs that nourish the vibrant life of the church and its people·

What We Are Doing

BOOKS | PARACLETE PRESS BOOKS show the richness and depth of what it means to be Christian. While Benedictine spirituality is at the heart of who we are and all that we do, our books reflect the Christian experience across many cultures, time periods, and houses of worship.

We have many series, including *Paraclete Essentials*; *Paraclete Fiction*; *Paraclete Poetry*; *Paraclete Giants*; and for children and adults, *All God's Creatures*, books about animals and faith; and *San Damiano Books*, focusing on Franciscan spirituality. Others include *Voices from the Monastery* (men and women monastics writing about living a spiritual life today), *Active Prayer*, and new for young readers: *The Pope's Cat*. We also specialize in gift books for children on the occasions of Baptism and First Communion, as well as other important times in a child's life, and books that bring creativity and liveliness to any adult spiritual life.

The MOUNT TABOR BOOKS series focuses on the arts and literature as well as liturgical worship and spirituality; it was created in conjunction with the Mount Tabor Ecumenical Centre for Art and Spirituality in Barga, Italy.

Music | The PARACLETE RECORDINGS label represents the internationally acclaimed choir *Gloriæ Dei Cantores*, the *Gloriæ Dei Cantores Schola*, and the other instrumental artists of the *Arts Empowering Life Foundation*.

Paraclete Press is the exclusive North American distributor for the Gregorian chant recordings from St. Peter's Abbey in Solesmes, France. Paraclete also carries all of the Solesmes chant publications for Mass and the Divine Office, as well as their academic research publications.

In addition, PARACLETE PRESS SHEET MUSIC publishes the work of today's finest composers of sacred choral music, annually reviewing over 1,000 works and releasing between 40 and 60 works for both choir and organ.

Video | Our video/DVDs offer spiritual help, healing, and biblical guidance for a broad range of life issues including grief and loss, marriage, forgiveness, facing death, understanding suicide, bullying, addictions, Alzheimer's, and Christian formation.

Learn more about us at our website: www.paracletepress.com, or call us toll-free at 1-800-451-5006.

SCAN TO READ MORE

you may also be interested in...

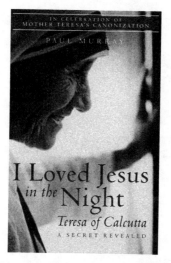

I Loved Jesus in the Night
Teresa of Calcutta — A Secret Revealed
Paul Murray

ISBN 978-1-61261-895-1 | $11.99

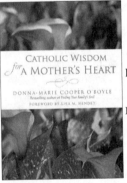